To:

From:

Illustrations copyright © 1998 Jacqueline Mair
This edition copyright © 1998 Lion Publishing

Published by
Lion Publishing plc
Sandy Lane West, Oxford, England
www.lion-publishing.co.uk
ISBN 0 7459 3997 X

First edition 1998
10 9 8 7 6 5 4 3 2
All rights reserved

A catalogue record for this book is available
from the British Library
Printed and bound in Singapore

Acknowledgments
We would like to thank all those who have given us
permission to include material in this book. Every
effort has been made to trace and acknowledge
copyright holders of all the quotations included.
We apologize for any errors or omissions that may
remain, and would ask those concerned to contact
the publishers, who will ensure that full
acknowledgment is made in the future.

All quotes by K. Bradford Brown © K. Bradford
Brown, published by Lifetimes Press.

Scriptures quoted from the *Good News Bible*
published by The Bible Societies/HarperCollins
Publishers Ltd, UK © American Bible Society,
1966, 1971, and 4th edition 1976.

♥ H E A R T F E L T S

Sisters

COMPILED BY FRANCES GRANT

LION
Giftlines

SISTERS

Sisters have a remarkable place in the fabric of human relationships, for it is with sisters that long-lasting links of affection, forgiveness, solidarity and balance are so often made. The words in this unique selection – from the most

sacred and ancient to
delightful glimpses from
the present day – reveal
sisterhood in its many
different forms. Yet they
all have loving bonds at
their centre. And they
mirror something far
greater: the loving bonds
of God.

♥

Something softens,
something leaps
forward, when I look
into the eyes of a
sister and see an
understanding heart.

SANNA KANE

The young ladies
entered the drawing
room in the full
fervour of sisterly
animosity.

R.S. SURTEES

Margaret glanced at her sister's note and pushed it over the breakfast-table to her aunt. There was a moment's hush, and then the flood-gates opened.

E.M. FORSTER

Lydia was Lydia still —
untamed, unabashed,
wild, noisy, and fearless.
She turned from sister
to sister, demanding
congratulation; and...
observed, with a laugh,
that it was a great while
since she had been there.

JANE AUSTEN

How different our lives
would be if we lived
them not as
physical beings on a
spiritual journey,
but as spiritual beings
on a physical journey.

UNKNOWN

'Lord, don't you care that my sister has left me to do all the work by myself? Tell her to come and help me!'

'Martha, Martha! You are worried and troubled over so many things... Mary has chosen the right thing, and it will not be taken away from her.'

FROM THE NEW TESTAMENT
GOSPEL OF LUKE

You tell your sister your secrets, you tell your sister you've scraped the car, you even tell your sister that you hate your sister (course, that bit's not true)— mainly because, you can tell your sister everything.

JAS NATHAN

Of course men can be sisters. We just call it something else, like mates. It's the same affection and companionship, with no ambition; the same joining of minds, with no pride. It's the same difference.

MICK YOUNG

Peace is not the
absence of conflict,
but the presence
of God.

K. BRADFORD BROWN

I never *asked* for my
sisters, they were just
there. I can still choose to
say yes, or no, to the
God-given in my life.
I *choose* to say *yes, yes*
I will love.

FRANCES GRANT

Whoever
does what
my father in
heaven wants him to do
is my brother, my sister,
and my mother.

FROM THE NEW TESTAMENT
GOSPEL OF MATTHEW

'Come! What gift would you like on your saint's day?' said Maria.

'You,' shrieked little Katya, delighted, 'You, you!'

And Maria was sad, for of all the presents she might give her sister, she herself could not be there.

RUSSIAN FOLK TALE

It is only the
women whose
eyes have been washed
clear with tears who
get the broad vision
that makes them little
sisters to all the
world.

DOROTHY DIX

A sister
is a great support-line.
As I have a sister,
I think they're
invaluable!

KATE FRASER

John Henderson, an
  unbeliever,
Had lately lost his
  joie de vivre…
Not so his sister,
  Mary Lunn,
She had a whacking
  lot of fun!

HILAIRE BELLOC

Too big, too small,
too fat, too thin,

too sweet, too sour,

too spiritual, too soppy.

Too everything,

my sister says.

Too much!

PHILIP CARTER

I am like this and
you are like that.
And vice versa.
As sisters with
completely different
natures, we're a pretty
amazing pair.

FRANCES GRANT

My sister and my
sister's child,
  Myself and
children three,
  Will fill the chaise;
so you must ride
  On horseback after we.

WILLIAM COWPER

♥

I know you what you are;
and, like a sister, am
most loath to call your
faults
as they are
named.

WILLIAM SHAKESPEARE

The two elder sisters were as ugly as carbuncles, though curiously each of them saw brute foulness only in the other. But the youngest of all, Cinderella, *was* beautiful; but through God's grace she did not know it.

FAIRY TALE

Treat wisdom
as your sister,
and insight as your
closest friend.

FROM THE OLD TESTAMENT
BOOK OF PROVERBS

She thought it wisest
to touch that point no
more. She knew her
sister's temper.

JANE AUSTEN

There's no friend like a sister, in calm or stormy weather, to cheer one on the tedious way... to strengthen whilst one stands.

CHRISTINA ROSSETTI

Sisters don't come
and go; sisters are
with you inside and
out, from the time
you were weaned to
the time you die.
*Boyfriends have nothing
on sisters.*

FRANNY HAMMONT

TOM: 'lease give me
my paintin' brush.
PETE: No.
TOM: *'lease* give me my
brush, or I get my big
sister.
PETE: No.
TOM (wailing):
Saraaaaaaaaaaaaaaaah!
PETE: OK then.

She was not going to
say, 'I love my dear
sister; I must
be near her at
this crisis in
her life.' The
affections are more
reticent than the
passions, and their
expression more subtle.

E.M. FORSTER

Sisterhood is one of God's best inventions. Where else do you find solid support, blaming your parents, and the dearest of frivolous nothings, in one and the same sentence?

HARRY WHYTE

'My dearest sister, now *be*, be serious. I want to talk very seriously, let me know everything I am to know, without delay!'

JANE AUSTEN

A garden
inclosed is

my sister.

FROM THE OLD TESTAMENT
SONG OF SONGS

The most important
thing women have to
do is to stir up the
zeal
of women
themselves.

JOHN STUART MILL

My teacher, my friend,
my instructor of many
loving ways – my
sister, my own dear
sister.

MARK STEPHENS

She is strong and
respected, and not
afraid of the future.

FROM THE OLD TESTAMENT
BOOK OF PROVERBS

What are the wild
waves saying
Sister, the whole day
long?

JOSEPH EDWARDS CARPENTER

As sisters
we are paid
daily for our life's work.
Our payment is
abundant life.

UNKNOWN